DEAD-LEAF MANTIS

TRICKS
Animals Play

By Jan Nagel Clarkson

BOOKS FOR YOUNG EXPLORERS
NATIONAL GEOGRAPHIC SOCIETY

The Opossum Plays Dead

HISS! The opossum tries to scare an enemy.
If the enemy does not go away,
the opossum falls down and plays dead.
When it lies very still, it is playing possum.
Then an enemy may leave it alone.
This is a trick that protects the opossum.
Other animals have unusual ways to get food
and to keep from being eaten.

Other Animals Pretend to Be Dead

The tiger moth plays dead too.
But it has another trick.
When it flops on its side,
an enemy can see
the orange color on its body.
The bright color is a warning.
It warns that this moth tastes BAD.
So its enemies stay away.

The hognose snake also protects itself by playing dead.
It rolls over on its back with its mouth wide open.
This snake is a very good bluffer. It doesn't move at all.
But if it is turned over, it will flop on its back again.

Some Animals Wear

The pangolin looks like a pinecone.
It is covered with hard scales.
When it rolls up into a ball,
the scales stick out. The scales have
sharp edges that can cut an enemy.

Hard Scales or Shells

The box turtle has a hard shell.
It can pull its head, legs, and tail
inside its shell.
Then the turtle is as safe and snug
as if it were inside a box.

The Hedgehog Changes into a Big Pincushion

The hedgehog has sharp quills
like a porcupine.
Quills are like needles —
almost as long as your little finger.
The hedgehog can curl itself into a prickly ball.
Then even a hungry enemy
may not attack the hedgehog.

These Animals Puff Up Like Balloons

A porcupine fish gulps water
when there is danger.
It puffs up, and sharp spines
stick out all over its body.
Do you think another fish
will try to swallow a puffed-up
porcupine fish?

This lizard gulps air
to make its body bigger.
And a beard pops out
below its mouth.
Then the lizard looks so scary
it may frighten an enemy away.

BEARDED LIZARD

These Animals Use Bad Smells to Keep Their Enemies Away

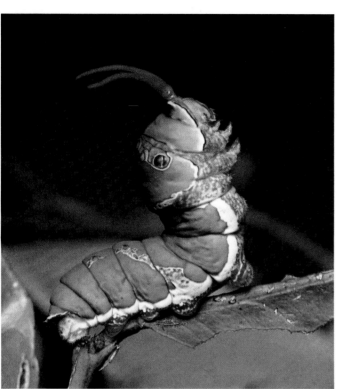

CATERPILLAR OF A CITRUS SWALLOWTAIL BUTTERFLY

With its tail raised high,
the skunk can spray an enemy.
The spray stings,
and it smells very, very bad.
This caterpillar and squash bug
also give off bad smells.
Enemies leave these animals alone.
They smell too bad to eat.

CATERPILLAR OF A HAWKMOTH

Looking Scary

If this caterpillar is in danger,
it bends way back.
Then it looks like a poisonous snake.
It cannot bite like a snake.
But the trick scares its enemies away.

Tricks
Moths Play

This moth looks like a hornet.
A hornet can sting.
Animals leave the moth alone,
because it looks like it can sting.

HORNET CLEARWING MOTH

This moth looks
like a bumblebee.
The moth has a fat, fuzzy body
that fools its enemies.

BUMBLEBEE HAWKMOTH

EUGLYPHIS MOTH

Is this a hairy spider
crawling up a tree trunk?
Look very carefully,
and you can see
the wings of this moth.

The Cuttlefish Has Many Tricks

When the cuttlefish is resting,
it looks like a rock.
Its round shape and light color
help it hide from enemies.
Hiding this way is called camouflage.
Camouflage protects animals
because it makes them hard to see.

As the cuttlefish swims
through the water,
it changes color.
Its color matches the pattern
of the ocean floor.

The cuttlefish can also change
its shape. It stretches out
and makes itself very flat.
This helps it move faster,
so it can escape an enemy.

Some Animals Scare
Their Enemies With Bright Colors

DEAD-LEAF MANTIS

A red light at the street corner tells you to STOP!
The red wings of this mantis seem to say STOP too.
Scientists think some animals use bright colors
to protect themselves. These bright colors
may help scare away their enemies.

The ring-necked snake curls up, and the enemy sees the orange tail.

The bark katydid lifts its wings to show the red color on its back.

As the crayfish gets ready to fight, it shows the red part of its claws.

Some Animals Protect
Their Babies in Special Ways

These baby fish hide in their mother's mouth.
The mother spits them out when it is safe.

The killdeer is a bird that pretends it is hurt
to lead an enemy away from its chick.
The bird drags one wing as if it were broken.
An enemy will follow because a hurt bird
is easy to catch. After the bird leads the enemy
far away, it flies back to its chick.

MOUTHBROODER FISH

The Cuckoo Tricks
the Warbler

The mother cuckoo waits in a tree
until the warbler leaves its nest.
Then the cuckoo lays one big egg
beside the two warbler eggs.
When the cuckoo hatches,
the little warbler brings food
to the big cuckoo chick.
The mother cuckoo has tricked
the warbler into feeding her chick.

Leaf-cutting Ants Grow Their Food

These ants carry pieces of leaves
to their nest underground.
The ants use the leaves
to grow a plant called fungus.

Fungus is a plant like a mushroom,
and it grows on the pile of leaves.
The fuzzy, white fungus
is the only food the ants ever eat.

In the ocean, there lives a fish called a decoy fish.
It uses a make-believe fish to catch little fish for its dinner.

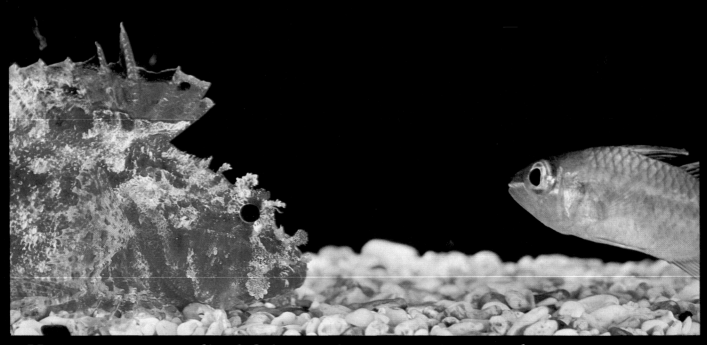

Here comes a cardinal fish. Maybe it is curious, or hungry too.

Believe Fish to Catch Its Dinner

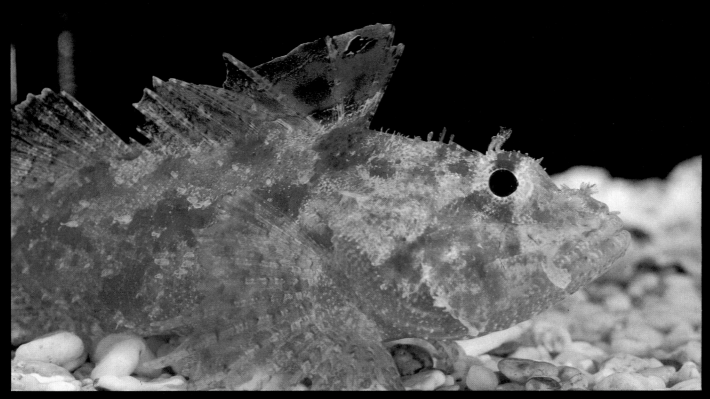

The decoy fish raises the fin on its back.
The fin has marks that look like an eye and the open mouth of a fish.

GULP! The trick works! The decoy fish swallows the cardinal fish.

A Fish That Goes Fishing

The frogfish has a fishing pole
above its mouth. As it waves the pole,
a little fish sees it and swims over.
Can you guess what happens
when the little fish swims near the pole?

A Fish That Goes Hunting

Do you see the beetle on the leaf?
The archerfish can knock the beetle
off the leaf by shooting drops of water at it.
This tricky fish uses its tongue
like a water gun.

Some Animals Use Tools

The chimpanzee sticks a blade of grass into a termite nest.
Then it eats the termites that bite the grass.
The sea otter pounds a clam on a rock to open it.
The grass and rock are tools that help the animals get food.
Once people did not believe animals used tools.
Don't you think these animals played a good trick on people?

Published by The National Geographic Society
Melvin M. Payne, *President;* Melville Bell Grosvenor, *Editor-in-Chief;* Gilbert M. Grosvenor, *Editor*

Prepared by
The Special Publications Division
Robert L. Breeden, *Editor*
Donald J. Crump, *Associate Editor*
Philip B. Silcott, *Senior Editor*
Cynthia Russ Ramsay, *Managing Editor*
Sallie M. Greenwood, *Research*

Illustrations
Geraldine Linder, *Picture Editor*

Design and Art Direction
Joseph A. Taney, *Staff Art Director*
Ursula Perrin, *Staff Designer*

Production and Printing
Robert W. Messer, *Production Manager*
George V. White, *Assistant Production Manager*
Raja D. Murshed, Nancy W. Glaser, *Production Assistants*
John R. Metcalfe, *Engraving and Printing*
Mary G. Burns, Jane H. Buxton, Stephanie S. Cooke, Suzanne J. Jacobson, Marilyn L. Wilbur,
Staff Assistants

Consultants
Dr. Glenn O. Blough, Peter L. Munroe, *Educational Consultants*
Edith K. Chasnov, *Reading Specialist*

Illustrations Credits

Edward S. Ross (1, 4, 6, 10 bottom, 12 bottom, 18, 19 center); L. G. Kesteloo, *National Audubon Society* (2); Stephen Collins, *National Audubon Society* (3); John Dommers, *Photo Researchers, Inc.* (4-5); Lynn M. Stone (7); E. Breeze Jones, *Bruce Coleman Inc.* (8); S. C. Bisserot, *Bruce Coleman Inc.* (9); Jane Burton, *Bruce Coleman Inc.* (10-11, 21); John R. Brownlie, *Bruce Coleman Inc.* (11 bottom); Anthony Bannister, *Natural History Photographic Agency* (12 top); Jen and Des Bartlett, *Bruce Coleman Inc.* (13, 15 top); N. Smythe (14 bottom); N. Smythe, *National Audubon Society* (14 top); C. J. Stine, *National Audubon Society* (15 center); Kjell B. Sandved (15 bottom); Carl Roessler, *Sea Library* (16, 17); Alan Blank, *Bruce Coleman Inc.* (19 top); Tom Myers (19 bottom); Jeff Foott, *Bruce Coleman Inc.* (20 top, 30); Joe Van Wormer, *Bruce Coleman Inc.* (20 bottom); Eric Hosking, *Bruce Coleman Inc.* (22 top); John Markham, *Bruce Coleman Inc.* (22 bottom, 23); Paul A. Zahl, *National Geographic Staff* (24-25); Ross E. Hutchins (25 top); Robert J. Schallenberger (26, 27, 28); Roy Pinney, *Photo Library Inc.* (29); Hugo van Lawick (31); Alan Root (32).

Cover Photograph: Jane Burton, *Bruce Coleman Inc.*

A WOODPECKER FINCH USES A CACTUS SPINE TO DIG FOR INSECTS